Make in a Day

PAPER FLOWERS

Amanda Evanston Freund

Dover Publications, Inc.
Mineola, New York

Bibliographical Note

Make in a Day: Paper Flowers is a new work,
first published by Dover Publications, Inc., in 2016.

Library of Congress Cataloging-in-Publication Data

Names: Freund, Amanda Evanston.
Title: Make in a day: paper flowers / Amanda Evanston Freund.
Description: Mineola, New York : Dover Publications, 2016.
Identifiers: LCCN 2016021136| ISBN 9780486810867 (paperback) |
    ISBN 0486810860 (paperback)
Subjects: LCSH: Paper work. | Decoration and ornament—Plant
    forms. | BISAC: CRAFTS & HOBBIES / Papercrafts. | CRAFTS &
    HOBBIES / Flower Arranging.
Classification: LCC TT870 .F73 2016 | DDC 736/.98—dc23 LC record
available at https://lccn.loc.gov/2016021136

Manufactured in the United States by RR Donnelley
81086001   2016
www.doverpublications.com

CONTENTS

In the winter of 1987, my father dropped me off at his mother's house for what was to be a life-altering afternoon. Theme colors made my Grandnanna Frances happy, and she carried this into the decorating of her house. The kitchen and living room were her favorite color—yellow—and it was because of a lack of yellow flowers in the store that winter that Grandnanna decided she would put me to work creating what would be the first of many thousands: paper flowers.

In the yellow kitchen she sat me down with a bowl of water, food coloring, thread, cellophane tape, wire hangers, and crunchy green wax paper, and for the next hour she directed me through the process of creating a coffee filter flower. *It was incredible!* While a series of small strokes had compromised the mobility of Grandnanna Frances's hands, they did not slow her tongue. Her knowledge of each step, to create every petal, every wrap of thread and wire, was directed toward me. This was not her making something with my assistance; this was me making something at her *insistence*. And I loved every moment of it! And, best of all, after a few flowers were finished, she picked the very best bloom and put it in her fanciest crystal vase and placed it up on the mantel. *The mantel!* A place reserved for oil paintings and exotic treasures was now home to my creation.

Since then, I have made it my business to learn how to make every paper flower under the sun and to share the journey with my readers. It is my sincerest hope that you will enjoy creating these blooms and share the fruits of your labor, or better, share the process with others. And if you are fortunate enough to make these flowers with a small child, I hope you will let them do the work. Then, take the flower, put it in a fancy vase and display it somewhere special where it can be admired. And one day, if the child is lucky, perhaps the flower of encouragement will blossom into something spectacular—perhaps one day that child will share their creativity with others just as I share mine with you now. My bloom started in a crystal vase on a mantel many, many years ago. Yours starts now.

Welcome to my garden!

Amanda Evanston Freund
AKA: Aunt Peaches
(Visit me at AuntPeaches.com)

Perfection is a dirty word—the joy is in the doing!

Hyacinths

The quintessential harbinger of spring, hyacinth bulbs bloom when the ground is still cold from winter frost and fade before Easter, not to be seen again for another year. Their moment to shine is far too brief! Although this project cannot replace the hyacinth's delicious scent, you can turn out dozens of these blooms in a single afternoon.

To make the hyacinths, you will need:

* Tissue paper
* Scissors
* Drinking straws
* Masking tape

Note
Each flower will require one piece of 3" x 36" tissue paper and one drinking straw.

1. Cut one strip of tissue paper, roughly 3" x 36" long, and fold in half lengthwise.

2. Fold in quarters and fringe the longest folded edge with scissors. Smooth flat when finished, keeping the folded edge intact.

3 Secure one end of tissue paper to the top 1" of a straw with a small piece of masking tape.

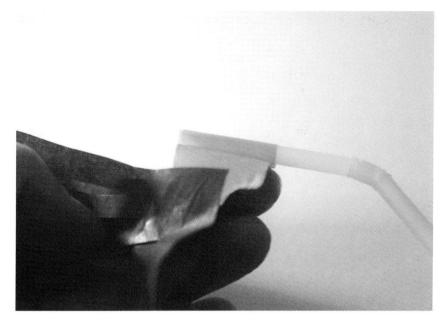

4 Roll the tissue diagonally down the length of the straw, gently pushing it upward on occasion until the flower is approximately 6" tall.

5 Secure the end of the fringed flower with masking tape and continue to wrap the masking tape downward.

Dandelions

Some people think dandelions are weeds but that's just a matter of perspective; they are *wildflowers*. They are cheerful. They are functional. They grow wherever they please. They aren't waiting for permission to grow. They don't need a greenhouse. They survive. They seed. They share. Interesting fact: the name dandelion comes from the shape of the leaves—*lion's teeth*. In France, they are called *pis-en-lit*, which roughly translates to "wet the bed." If you have ever had dandelion tea before bed, you'll know where that expression comes from!

To make the dandelions, you will need:

* Tissue paper
* Scissors
* Drinking straws
* Masking tape

Note
Each flower will require three pieces of 6" x 36" tissue paper.

1 Cut three sheets of tissue paper into three strips, roughly 6" x 36" long. All three sheets need to be the exact same size.

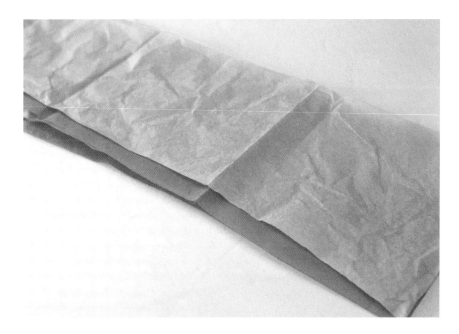

2 Fold in half, lengthwise.

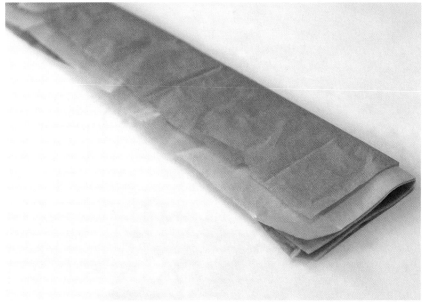

3 Fringe the folded edge of the tissue paper with scissors.

4 Fold the long strip in half, keeping the fringe intact.

5 Fold again and position the strips so the bottom edge of all the layers is exposed slightly.

6 Lay a 12" piece of masking tape across the base of the tissue and smooth with your fingers.

7 Snip off the folded tips of the fringe.

8 Attach the end of the masking tape to the tip of a drinking straw.

9 Roll the straw down the length of the masking tape; continue to roll the masking tape down the top third of the straw.

10 Flip over and fluff the petals with your fingers.

Hydrangeas

In nature, hydrangea flowers can grow as large as a head of cauliflower, with each flower composed of hundreds of smaller blooms in varying shades of color. Here we are re-creating the traditional blue on periwinkle hydrangea that is so beloved but difficult to grow at home. With this project, you can create hydrangeas in any color your heart desires.

To make the hydrangeas, you will need:

- ✳ Tissue paper in two similar color tones
- ✳ White tacky glue
- ✳ Drinking straws

- ✳ Scissors
- ✳ Masking tape
- ✳ Marker
- ✳ Scrap paper

Note
Each flower will require 20 circular tissue pieces for the petals.

1 Cut tissue paper into five 4" squares and fold all five pieces into quarters.

2 Use scissors to cut circles; this should yield twenty 2" circles.

3 Crumple one 4" square piece of tissue into a loose ball.

4 Wrap the ball with another 4" piece of tissue.

5 Use a 5" piece of masking tape to attach the ball to the top of the drinking straw. Wrap tightly.

6 Squeeze a tablespoon of glue onto a piece of scrap paper.

7 Pull the center of one piece of tissue over the blunt end of a thick marker.

8 Dip the tissue gently into the glue, still holding it over the end of the marker.

9 Use the marker to tap the tissue circles onto the ball, starting toward the bottom of the ball.

10 Working from the bottom up, repeat Step 9, continuing to add tissue pieces as you go. Twenty circles will cover the sphere nicely, but feel free to add texture with additional circles or add a second layer, alternating colors as you go.

Snapdragons

Growing taller than most flowers, snapdragons stand proudly vertical above the rest. With their giraffe-like proportions, it is interesting that they were named for dragons because when an individual blossom is squeezed, it opens and closes its mouth like a dragon. *Oh snap!* Unfortunately, these tissue paper blooms do not open and close their mouths, but they sure do make for a stunning display!

To make the snapdragons, you will need:

* Crepe paper streamers

* Tissue paper similar in color to the crepe paper streamers

* White tacky glue

* Drinking straw or small dowel

* Masking tape

* Scissors

Note

Each flower stalk will require at least 15 blossoms. If you don't have an extra long drinking straw, tape two straws together or use a wooden dowel. Masking tape that has been sliced to less than ¾" thick will be especially useful for this project.

1 Fold a 30" piece of streamer repeatedly until it is 3" long. Fringe one edge of the streamer with scissors leaving the opposite edge intact.

2 Unfold the long strip and slice into 2" pieces.

3 Pinch the non-fringed side of the streamer and twist.

4 Layer multiple sheets of tissue paper and trace 2", 3", and 4" circles. Keeping multiple sheets of tissue stacked, cut out the circles. The end goal is to cut out at least 15 circles of varying sizes.

5 Squeeze several small dots of glue in the center of one circle.

6 Insert the tuft of fringed streamer into the center of a tissue circle and pinch.

7 Repeat gluing, inserting, and pinching until at least 15 blossoms are made.

8 Wrap the entire length of a straw with masking tape.

9 Starting at the top, adhere masking tape to the straw, spiraling from top to bottom while inserting blossoms along the way. Insert smaller blossoms toward the top, larger blossoms at the bottom.

10 Secure the final blossom and continue spiraling downward.

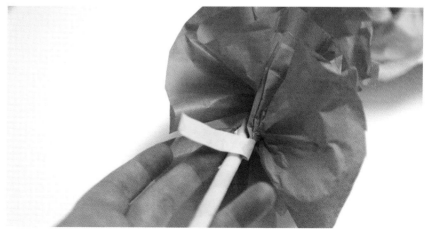

Camellias

Beloved by fashion designer Coco Chanel, the camellia has long stood as an icon of high-end design. Here it is again, reinterpreted in paper, in a deceptively simple craft project. Use a camellia as a gift topper, birthday badge, or refrigerator magnet, or make dozens to go around a wreath.

To make the camellias, you will need:

* * Tissue paper in two colors (or more)
* * White tacky glue
* * Scissors

Note
Each camellia requires six large and two small circles of tissue paper. This project can easily be upsized by doubling the size and quantity of the circles.

1 Fold large sheets of tissue paper and trace two different-sized circles on the top sheet.

2 Cut out circles. You will want six large circles and two small circles per flower.

3 With the exception of one small circle for each of the flowers, add two or three dots of glue toward the center of each of the circles; try to avoid placing the glue in the exact center.

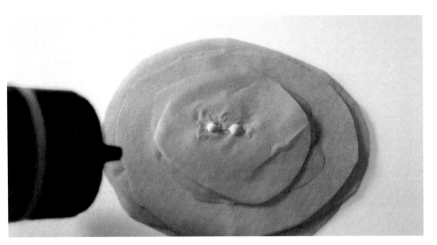

4 Layer all the larger circles on top of each other, with a few slightly off-center for added dimension. Follow with the smaller circles.

5 Add the final (unglued) small circle to the top of the circles.

6 Allow the glue to dry at least 30 minutes.

7 Pull the topmost circle upward, rumpling the edges toward the center, then follow with the other small circles.

8 Pinch the larger circles up slightly, one by one, ruffling the edges as needed.

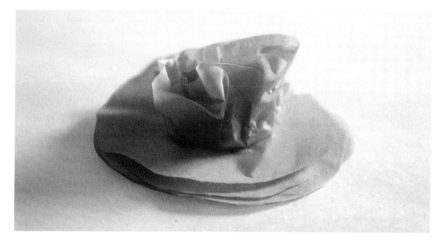

9 Secure to a pin back or a magnet, or tie to the top of a special gift.

Teacup Roses

Named for the cup-like bowl that surrounds their intensely ruffled inner blooms, teacup-style roses are beloved by traditional English garden enthusiasts all over the world. Their blossoms can often be found etched in the borders of vintage dishes and tablewear—and with this project you can make a centerpiece to match!

To make the teacup roses, you will need:

* Coffee filters pre-dyed and dried (see page 60)
* Tissue paper similar in color to the coffee filters
* Drinking straws
* Masking tape
* Scissors

Note
Each rose will require six coffee filters and one 6" x 36" piece of tissue paper.

1. Pinch one filter in the direct center, forming a gentle cone shape. Set aside.

2. Continue to pinch filters until you have the desired quantity (six filters per rose).

3 Lay a 6" piece of masking tape and attach it to the top 1" of a drinking straw. One by one, add the tips of the coffee filters to the tape, sticking as you go. Leave at least 2" of exposed tape at the end.

4 Roll the straw across the filters tightly.

5 Wrap the remaining tape around the bundle and secure as tightly as possible.

6 Accordion fold one piece of 6" x 36" tissue paper. Curve off one end with your scissors.

7 Unfold the tissue; you will have a scalloped edge.

8 Secure the tissue to the top of the straw using masking tape, aiming to have the tops of the scallops just slightly higher than the edges of the coffee filters.

9 Gently roll the tissue around the bundle of coffee filters.

10 Tightly wrap the base of the tissue with masking tape. Continue down the straw if desired.

Water Lilies

They say you have never truly lived until you have been to Paris. We can conjure up some Parisian flair with a nod to a work by the city's favorite son—Claude Monet, and his water lilies. Scattered across a table or on top of a simple gift, these water lilies add a festive touch!

To make the water lilies, you will need:

* Extra large baking cups
* Tissue paper

* White tacky glue
* Scissors

Note
Each flower will require five baking cups and two circles of tissue paper. If extra large baking cups are not available, you can supersize this project using plain white coffee filters. Using very small amounts of fast-drying, extra thick white glue will prove very helpful for this project.

1 Fold two 4" squares of tissue paper into quarters and round off the corner to create a circle.

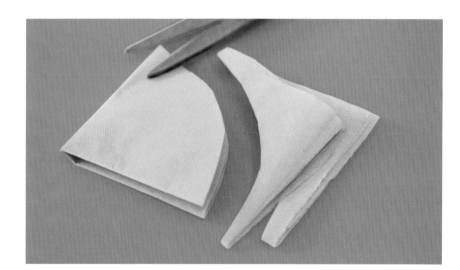

2 Fringe the circle along the edge, leaving the center intact.

3 Unfold the circles and separate the edges.

4 Stack five baking cups and fold three times into eighths.

5 Use scissors to cut a rounded point into the outer edge.

6 Unfold the baking cups to reveal an eight-point flower.

7 Pull the baking cups apart and squeeze four small dots of glue into the center of one baking cup. Press the bottom of another baking cup onto the glue dots. Repeat with all five baking cups, alternating petal points as you go.

8 Squeeze more glue dots to attach the two fringed circles to the center of the baking cups and allow the glue to firm up, at least 15 minutes.

9 Gently pull the two fringed circles upward, pinching slightly at the base.

10 Continue to pull the other layers upward making the flower as full and fluffy as possible.

Clematis

The clematis is a vine flower popular all over the world for its hardy nature and showy blooms. For this project, you can enjoy a single stem in a simple vase, or scatter a handful across a table or up a winding reed. Paper flowers like this make it easy to enjoy clematis from the comfort of home.

To make the clematis, you will need:

* Tissue paper
* Crepe paper streamers
* Drinking straws
* Masking tape
* Scissors

Note
Each flower will require three 6" squares of tissue paper.

1. Cut a 16" piece of streamer, fold in quarters, and fringe the long edge with scissors, leaving the bottom ½" intact.

2. Use a 2" piece of tape to attach one end of the streamer to the top of a drinking straw.

3 Roll the streamer around the end of the straw and secure with another small piece of tape.

4 Stack three 6" square pieces of tissue paper and fold into quarters. Use scissors to cut loose petal shapes around the edge.

5 Unfold the flower and snip an incision in the center slightly larger than the width of the drinking straw.

6 Open and flatten the flowers.

7 Insert the bottom of the straw through the incision in the center of the flower and gently pull toward the top. Repeat with the other two tissue flowers and bundle loosely. Use masking tape to tightly wrap the bottom base of the flower.

8 Continue to wrap the straw to make the stem.

9 Pull back the petals to shape your flower.

Color-Splotched Dahlias

The national flower of Mexico, the dahlia was discovered by the Aztec Indians centuries ago. First appreciated for their medicinal purposes, dahlias were later cultivated for their appearance, eventually morphing into every shape, color, and size imaginable. Some dahlias grow stout and spherical, while others bloom wide and flat—as large as dinner plates! Their variety is only surpassed by their beauty, so it is appropriate that this project capitalizes on the limitless possibilities of tie dye. No two of these blooms will ever be alike!

To make the color-splotched dahlias, you will need:

* Coffee filters
* Pipe cleaners
* Tissue paper
* Drinking straws
* Watercolor paints
* Paintbrush

Note

Each flower will require four coffee filters and one drinking straw. Some brands of coffee filters will be extra starchy and the watercolor will not sink through all four layers—the easiest remedy for this is to dip the stack of filters in water first, then wring out the excess moisture *before* painting.

1 Separate coffee filters into stacks of four and paint with dabbles of watercolor paint. Dry thoroughly. The watercolor should dye all four coffee filters. Take the stack of four filters and fold into quarters.

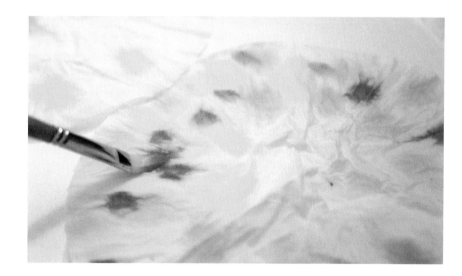

2 Cut four to six finger-like petals along the edge of the filters.

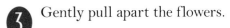
3 Gently pull apart the flowers.

4 Stack three 4" squares of tissue paper and fold into quarters. Round off one corner with scissors.

5 Fringe around the edge and unfold.

6 Fold one pipe cleaner in half and poke the pointed ends through the center of one of the tissue paper circles, with the two holes set 1" apart. Repeat with the other two pieces of tissue paper.

7 Poke the ends of the pipe cleaner through the center of one coffee filter with the two holes set 1" apart. Repeat with the other three coffee filters. Pull all of the coffee filters upward and bundle loosely.

8 Use a 4" piece of masking tape to tightly wrap the base of the flower as well as the top of the folded pipe cleaner.

9 Insert the pipe cleaner into a drinking straw and wrap both the straw and flower base with one continuous piece of masking tape.

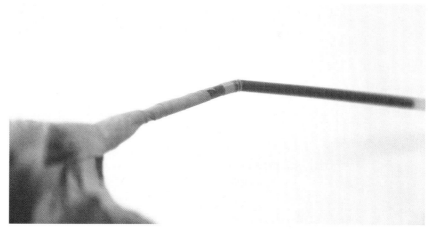

10 Gently fluff the petals.

Technicolor Chrysanthemums

Leftover artwork is the thorn in the side for artists of all ages. And as any parent of young children can tell you, the refrigerator art gallery is short on real estate and high in demand. So what do you do with all that leftover artwork? Turn it into flowers, either to be given away or collected and displayed lovingly at home. This project breathes life into paper goods that would often go unnoticed at the bottom of a drawer and turns them into something worth celebrating!

To make the technicolor chrysanthemums, you will need:

* Painted paper artwork
* Drinking straws
* Scissors
* Masking tape

Note
Each flower will require one piece of paper, any size. If the art piece is single-sided, you may want to consider using a marker or crayon to create a simple pattern on the underside before creating the flower.

1 Cut the art piece in half, lengthwise.

2 Stack both pieces of paper, front side up, and fold in half, lengthwise.

3 Use scissors to fringe the edges.

4 Lay the two long pieces side by side and secure them to each other with a piece of masking tape.

5 Attach the bottom ½" of the strip to the top ½" of the straw with a small piece of masking tape.

6 Roll the straw along the length of the masking tape, keeping the paper in a neat and level line.

7 Secure the end of the strip with a 5" piece of masking tape and continue to wrap along the base and onto the top of the drinking straw.

8 Gently pull back the petals, starting at the outermost layers, spiraling toward the center.

9 Gently fluff the petals.

Roses

By far the most popular flower on the planet, roses are a universal favorite. Fragrant, long-lasting, and easy on the eyes, what more could you want from a flower? Interestingly, traditional long-stemmed roses must often be grown in tubes or cylindrical cages in order to achieve their tall and lengthy appearance, making them not quite so natural as you might expect. Their chubby and lighthearted sisters, garden roses, take a more casual approach to life. With paper roses, you might miss the scent, but the only limit to the size and color of the bloom is your imagination.

To make the roses, you will need:

- Dyed coffee filters (see page 60 for directions)
- Pencil

- Pipe cleaners
- Drinking straws
- Scissors

Note
Each flower will require six coffee filters.

1. Stack six filters and fold in half, then in thirds. Round off the corners with scissors.

2. Unfold the filters and use scissors to make incisions between each rounded petal, leaving the center 2" intact.

3 Lay a pencil at the very end of one petal, keeping the stack of six filters shuffled together.

4 Roll the pencil toward the center of the flower, taking all six filters along.

5 Pinch two fingers on either side of the petal and push inward. To make it easier, you may want to loosen the rolled filters slightly. Repeat the rolling and pinching process along all six petals.

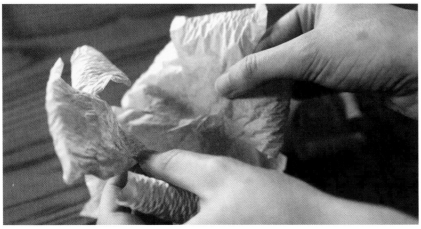

6 Gently pull the filters apart, keeping away from the edges. Do *not* touch the curled edges.

7 Bend a pipe cleaner in half and poke the two pointed ends through the center of one filter with the holes spaced 1" apart.

8 Continue inserting filters as you go, alternating the placement of the petals with every layer.

9 Twist the base of the pipe cleaner. Fluff petals gently, keeping the curl intact.

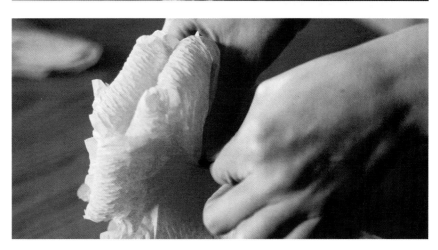

10 Squeeze a thin line of glue along the twisted pipe cleaner and slide into a decorative drinking straw.

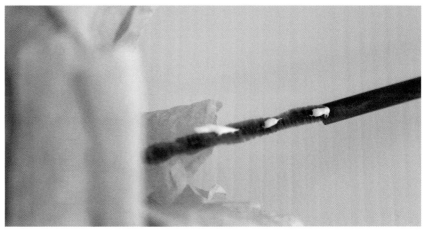

Daffodils

A beloved symbol of the Irish countryside, daffodils flourish in unusual and wild places, turning up in gardens and on roadsides alike. Daffodil season lasts but a month in early spring, but with this project you can enjoy their architectural, trumpet-like blooms as a happy addition to your home anytime.

To make the daffodils, you will need:

* Large baking cups
* Small baking cups
* Drinking straws

* White tacky glue
* Scissors
* Large marker

Note
Each daffodil will require one large baking cup and one small baking cup.
Straws with elbow bends are recommended for this particular flower.

1 Fold one large baking cup in half and then in thirds.

2 Cut a triangle with the point ending in the center, outer edge.

3 Unfold the baking cup; it will loosely resemble a six-point star.

4 Pinch the center of the baking cup and twist, forming a stub about ½" long.

5 Squeeze some glue directly into the end of the straw closest to the elbow.

6 Insert the stub of the large baking cup into the now glue-filled end of the straw.

7 Pull the small baking cup over the blunt end of a large marker.

8 Add a dab of glue to the center of the small baking cup.

9 Place your finger inside the center of the small baking cup, flip, and place in the direct center of the large baking cup.

10 Use your finger to thoroughly adhere the center of the small baking cup to the large one.

Tie-Dyed Tulips

Tulips are a long-beloved symbol of spring. So prized for their appearance, tulip bulbs were used as currency in the Netherlands centuries ago. And while they come in a variety of sizes and colors, tulip season lasts for only a few weeks a year. With this version made from coffee filters, you can enjoy them throughout every season and in every shade of the rainbow—*literally*.

To make the tie-dyed tulips, you will need:

* Cone-shaped coffee filters

* Markers

* Drinking straws

* Spray bottle filled with water

* White tacky glue

Note

The tie-dyeing process relies on water-soluble markers, which are usually the least expensive and easiest to find. Alcohol-based, permanent markers will not work for this project. Because the filters may bleed some ink in the drying process, an old towel or an underlay of paper towels is recommended.

1   Using markers, doodle over the surface of the coffee filter, including the edges.

2   With a layer of towels underneath, spray the coffee filter with water until it is nearly saturated.

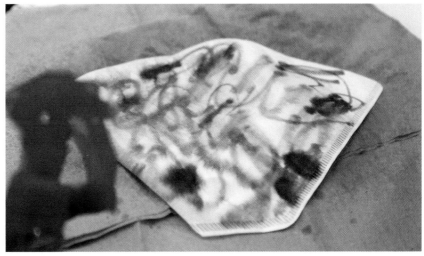

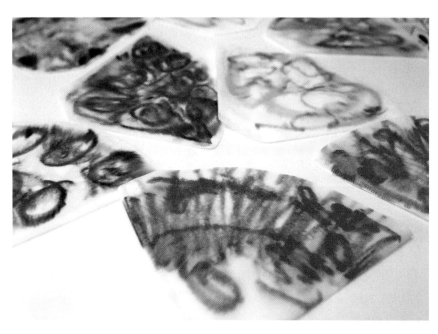

3 Watch the colors of the ink slowly bleed into each other as you allow them to dry.

4 Fold the filter five times, accordion style.

5 Snip a triangle into the outer edge of the filter.

6 Twist the bottom 1" of the filter, forming a small stub. Be careful not to tear it off completely.

7 Squeeze a generous amount of glue onto the stub at the base.

8 Insert the stub into the top of a drinking straw.

Poppies

It is hard to imagine a flower as happy as a poppy. Each morning poppies open their beach umbrella–like petals and raise their faces to the sun, only to close their umbrellas again each night. Wild poppies can grow in prolific, weed-like quantities, taking over entire fields and farms. And, while this project might not turn out in such a large scale, after making one, you will want to dive in and make a hundred more. These flowers could not be easier, and the results are utterly impressive.

To make the poppies, you will need:

* Tissue paper, two solid colors and one pattern

* Masking tape

* Drinking straws

* Scissors

Note
You may find it helpful to keep white tacky glue on hand to connect petal gaps.

1. Fold a 3" x 10" piece of patterned tissue paper in quarters and fringe one edge.

2. Cut two 6" squares of solid-colored tissue and crumple one of them into a ball.

3 Use the remaining 6" square to cover the crumpled ball of tissue and twist off the bottom.

4 Secure the stem of the tissue ball to the top of a drinking straw by tightly wrapping it in a long spiral of masking tape.

5 Roll the base of the ball in the 10" length of tissue paper and secure with another stretch of masking tape, wrapping as tightly as possible. Fluff open the petals.

6 Cut two 7" x 36" pieces of tissue paper and use your fingers to pinch the entire length of the paper, accordion style. Allow the paper to relax, making sure the folding is fairly consistent.

7 Lay a 4" piece of masking tape on a table, sticky side up. Use your fingers to scrunch one piece of the tissue down to less than 2" and adhere it to one side of the masking tape. Repeat with the other piece of tissue so they lie side by side, leaving a small amount of tape on either end.

8 Place the base of the fringed ball at one tip of the tape and secure with additional masking tape if needed. Roll up tightly.

9 Wrap the bottom 1" of the base with additional tape, spiraling down the straw as you desire.

10 Gently pull back the petals and admire your work.

Peonies

The peony is one of the largest and most beloved of all the flowers in the garden. Peonies are named after Paean, a student under the Greek God of medicine, Asclepius. When the student grew more knowledgeable than his teacher, Zeus saved Paean from Asclepius's wrath by turning him into a flower, which resembles what we now call a peony. Appropriately, compounds taken from peonies and their stems are widely used to create medical treatments and pharmaceuticals, helping to treat a slew of conditions, including fever, gout, and respiratory illnesses. Peonies are far more than just a pretty face!

To make the peonies, you will need:

- ✳ Coffee filters
- ✳ Tissue paper
- ✳ Food coloring
- ✳ Two bowls of water
- ✳ Masking tape
- ✳ Pipe cleaners
- ✳ Scissors
- ✳ Drinking straws

Note
Each flower will require seven filters and three small circles of tissue. These instructions are designed to achieve a two-tone blossom, but you can bypass the first two steps by dyeing your filters a solid color according to the steps on page 60.

1 Squeeze 10 drops of food coloring into one cup of water. Mix thoroughly. Form a stack of seven filters into a loose cone shape and dip at least 2" of the outer edges into a clean bowl of water. Make sure the outer edges are fully saturated. Flip the bundle of filters, pinch by the wet outer edges, then dip the pointed center in the dyed water. Wring out excess moisture.

2 Flatten the filters and check to see that the dye penetrated all seven layers. It is normal for the top layer to be much more vibrant than the bottom layers. Dry filters thoroughly, either singly or in stacks of seven, which will take longer.

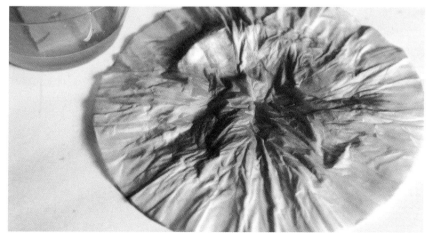

3 Fold the filters in quarters. Slice pointed petals along the outer edge of the filters.

4 Cut three 4" circles of tissue paper. Fold the circles in quarters and fringe the edges. Unfold the circles and gently pull apart layers.

5 Bend one pipe cleaner in half and insert the pointed ends through a single layer of tissue paper, in the center, 1" apart. Follow with the two other layers of tissue.

6 Insert the pointed ends through a single coffee filter, in the center, 1" apart. Pull upward, forming a gentle cone shape over the three layers of tissue paper. Repeat with the other six coffee filters, keeping the most vibrantly colored filters as the top layers. Push all ten layers (seven filters, three tissue circles) toward the top and pinch the base.

7 Twist the pipe cleaners together.

8 Add a thin line of glue along one side of the twisted pipe cleaner.

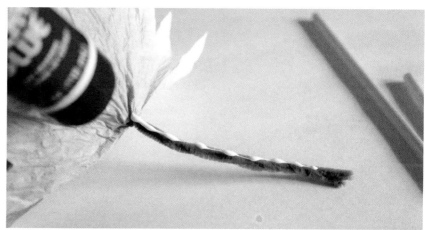

9 Slide the twisted pipe cleaner into a drinking straw, swirling slightly as you go to help spread the glue.

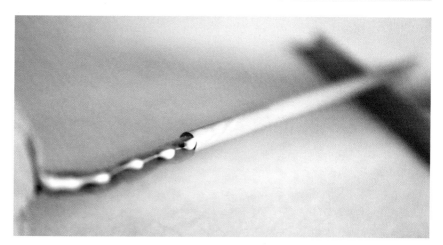

10 With a 10" piece of masking tape, tightly wrap bottom 1" of flower, spiraling down the length of the straw. To make a longer stem, pinch the end of a second straw, insert it into the bottom of the first straw and continue wrapping the tape down. Then, gently fluff and pull the edges of the flower, exposing the tissue paper center.

Dyeing Filters

Coffee filters pose an unusual solution to a variety of crafting needs. While they are lightweight and extremely inexpensive, they are also very sturdy. Made of a composite of cotton fibers and starch, coffee filters are a 9" circle of paper with all the flexibility of fabric. The bad news is they only come in two colors: white and brown. The good news is they are easy to dye using regular food coloring. Depending on the brand, usually a few drops added to a cup of water will do the trick. Want more vibrant tones? Add a splash of vinegar. Most food coloring manufacturers offer an index of color recipes on the side of the box for dyeing Easter eggs—you'll find these recipes and rations are ideal for dyeing dozens of coffee filters. Just pinch off a stack of ten and dip them in—no need to let them soak, the color will adhere in a matter of moments.

Drying Filters

Drying coffee filters in short stacks hung over a towel bar or laundry line is easy but it can take hours. This is fine for small batches, but if you're dyeing hundreds of filters at the same time, just throw them into a dryer with an old towel on high heat for five minutes—they will come out nicely textured and piping hot! With the dryer method, be careful to avoid mixing filters dyed from opposite colors or they may stain each other in the tumbling process.

Dyeing Other Items

Tissue paper, crepe paper, streamers, and even newsprint can all be dyed to any color you wish. Just be careful to dip them quickly as some paper will fall apart and melt if left in the water too long!